THIS
BELONGS TO

Manufactured by Amazon.ca
Bolton, ON

53122002R00072